ALEX MORGAN

Abbeville Press Publishers

New York · London

A portion of the proceeds from this book are donated to the **Hugo Bustamante AYSO Playership Fund**, a national scholarship program to help ensure that no child misses the chance to play AYSO Soccer. Donations to the fund cover the cost of registration and a uniform for a child in need.

Text by Illugi Jökulsson

For the original edition
Design: Ólafur Gunnar Guðlaugsson
Layout: Ólafur Gunnar Guðlaugsson and Árni Torfason

For the English-language edition
Editor: Nicole Lanctot
Production manager: Louise Kurtz
Layout: Ada Rodriguez
Copy editor: Carrie Bebris

PHOTOGRAPHY CREDITS

Getty Images: p. 2 (Stanley Chou), 4 (Stanley Chou), 9 (Patrick Smith), 10 (Alex: Martin Rose), 10 (Berlin Wall: Gamma-Rapho), 11 (Maradona: Michael King), 12 (Tiffany: Han Myung-Gu), 12 (Dev: Brian Ach), 14 (Brett Carlsen), 16 (Topical Press Agency), 17 (Sun Wen: Lars Baron), 17 (Marta: Popperfoto), 19 (Robert Beck), 20 (Akers: Aubrey Washington), 20 (Lilly: Elsa), 21 (Hamm: Shaun Botterill), 20 (Milbrett: Jonathan Ferrey), 23 (Anna Webber), 25 (Large: Jonathan Ferrey), 25 (Small: Martin Bernetti/AFP), 26 (Alexandra Beier), 28 (Martin Rose), 30 (Marta: Popperfoto), 30 (Hamm: Elsa), 30 (Alex: Doug Pensinger), 30 (Solo: Cooper Neill), 32 (Stuart Franklin), 33 (Thorsten Wagner), 37 (Rich Lam), 39 (Stanley Chou), 41 (Ronald Martinez), 42 (Ali: Hulton Archive), 45 (Top: Stanley Chou), 47 (Dave Kotinsky), 48 (Left: Jon Kopaloff), 48 (Right: Mike Windle), 49 (Thomas Concordia), 52 (Robert Cianflone), 53 (Leroux: Patrick Smith), 53 (Rodriguez: Martin Rose), 53 (Press: Michael Campanella), 54 (Solo: Jared Wickerham), 54 (Rapinoe: Andrew Yates/AFP), 55 (Rampone: Leon Halip), 56 (David Madison), 59 (Victor Decolongon), 63 (Kevin C. Cox)

Shutterstock: p. 12 (Diamond Bar: trekandshoot), 12 (Snoop Dogg: Mat Hayward), 20 (EKS), 30 (Ronaldo: Natursport), 30 (Messi: mooinblack), 43 (Beyoncé: Everett Collection), 43 (Beach: Anton Gvozdikov), 43 (Alex: Leon Halip), 44 (Leopard: Stayer), 44 (Goulding: Jaguar PS), 44 (Howard: Featureflash), 44 (Doctor: wavebreakmedia), 45 (Center: Andrea Haase)

Wikimedia Commons: p. 10 (Bush Reagan), 17 (Prinz: Heinrich-Böll-Stiftung), 18 (Foudy: RyanDowIMG), 18 (Fawcett: Johnmaxmena2), 45 (Morgan: Ampatent), 54 (O'Reilly: Ampatent), 53 (Heath: Pierre-Yves Beaudouin), 54 (Cheney: Ampatent), 54 (Boxx: Ampatent), 55 (Sauerbrunn: Ampatent), 55 (Krieger: Hobgoodc), 55 (Klingenberg: Am patent), 55 (O'Hara: Ampatent), 55 (Buehler: BrokenSphere), 57 (Carrasco: Noah Salzman)

Isiphotos: p. 34 (Brad Smith)

Youtube: p. 15 (USSoccer)

First published in the United States of America in 2015 by Abbeville Press, 137 Varick Street, New York, NY 10013

First published in Iceland in 2014 by Sögur útgáfa, Fákafen 9, 108 Reykjavík, Iceland

First edition
10 9 8 7 6 5 4 3 2 1

Library of Congress Cataloging-in-Publication Data

Illugi Jökulsson.
  [Alex Morgan. English]
  Alex Morgan / Illugi Jvkulsson.
    pages cm. — (World soccer legends)
    Summary: "Recounts the story of American soccer star Alex Morgan, one of the best female players in the world. The book tracks her success in helping to win the FIFA World Cup, a team gold medal in the 2012 Olympics, and her achievements outside of soccer, including writing and modeling"— Provided by publisher.
  ISBN 978-0-7892-1216-0 (hardback)
  1. Morgan, Alex (Alexandra Patricia), 1989—Juvenile literature. 2. Women soccer players—United States—Biography—Juvenile literature. 3. Soccer players—United States—Biography—Juvenile literature. I. Title.
  GV942.7.M673I5513 2015
  796.334092—dc23
  [B]
                         2014045290

For bulk and premium sales and for text adoption procedures, write to Customer Service Manager, Abbeville Press, 137 Varick Street, New York, NY 10013, or call 1-800-Artbook.

Visit Abbeville Press online at www.abbeville.com.

CONTENTS

ALEX MORGAN

THE NEW AMERICAN STAR

The 2015 Women's World Cup will be held in Canada. The United States Women's National Team has proven itself to be one of the world's most powerful soccer teams in the last 25 years. FIFA* ranks USA in first place, a position it has held since early 2008. The team won the gold medal in the past three Summer Olympics, for a total of four gold medals overall since women's soccer became an Olympic sport in 1996. This triumphant march is slightly stalled by one fact: USA has failed to win the World Cup since 1999.

This may be about to change! USA heads to Canada with an extremely strong team. The player who makes the difference this time and ensures USA the sought-after World Cup title might be the young and tremendously skillful Alex Morgan. She is the most recent wonder in a long line of women's soccer superstars, and it will hardly be surprising if Morgan becomes the catalyst that brings about victory for the U.S. team in Canada.

* The International Football Association. See glossary, page 60.

OTHER EVENTS OF 1989

In July, President George H.W. Bush had held office for six months, after succeeding Ronald Reagan in January.

In June, student protests in Beijing's Tiananmen Square came to a tragic end when government troops killed thousands of unarmed protesters. Positive events also took place: the oppressive communist regimes in Middle and Eastern Europe collapsed in the autumn.

BORN ON THE 2ND OF JULY 1989

November 9: The Berlin Wall comes tumbling down.

CANCER & SNAKE!

Alex Morgan's zodiac sign is Cancer, according to Western astrology. Individuals born under the Cancer sign are supposedly loyal and dependable, especially when it comes to their family, friends, and loved ones, but they are also a bit prone to mood swings!

According to Chinese astrology, Morgan is born in the year of the Snake. In China, this is not considered negative in any way because snakes are seen as highly intelligent creatures. Morgan's Chinese element is Earth. Her modern birthstone is the ruby, whereas her Zodiac birthstone is the emerald.

Note: Astrology can be a lot of fun, but it has no scientific basis.

FILMS OF THE YEAR

The worldwide highest-grossing film of 1989 was the third installment in the Indiana Jones series, *Indiana Jones and the Last Crusade*, starring Harrison Ford and Sean Connery. *Indiana Jones* was followed by *Batman*, starring Michael Keaton, with Jack Nicholson in the role of the Joker. Other popular films that year were *Back to the Future Part II*, *Look Who's Talking*, *Dead Poets Society*, and Disney's *The Little Mermaid*.

Driving Miss Daisy won the Academy Award for Best Picture. *Born on the Fourth of July*, directed by Oliver Stone, also garnered numerous awards.

MARADONA

Argentina, led by Diego Maradona, was the reigning world champion in men's soccer after winning the 1986 World Cup in Mexico.

Costa Rica became CONCACAF* soccer champions in 1989, closely followed by USA. Both teams qualified for the 1990 FIFA Men's World Cup, USA qualifying for the first time since 1950.

* See glossary, page 60.

THE BIGGEST HIT SINGLES OF 1989

1. Madonna: *Like a Prayer*
2. The Bangles: *Eternal Flame*
3. Phil Collins: *Another Day in Paradise*

DIAMOND BAR

Alex Morgan was born in Diamond Bar, a California city close to Los Angeles. From Diamond Bar it takes about 45 minutes to drive to central Los Angeles. The land on which Diamond Bar stands was once home to a ranch. In 1847, the rancher at the time passed away and his widow sold the land in exchange for 100 calves, $100 in merchandise, and payment of the husband's debts. Farming continued on the land until the 1950s when a large corporation bought the land to develop a residential area. The new city grew quickly and was incorporated in 1989. It is named after the diamond-over-a-bar branding iron symbol registered in 1918 by ranch owner Frederick E. Lewis.

SNOOP DOGG

The most famous resident of Diamond Bar is rapper Snoop Dogg. He moved from downtown Los Angeles to the quiet and affluent little city in the hills to give his sons a normal high school experience.

Snoop Dogg

In 2014 the population of Diamond Bar was 55,500.

Tiffany

TIFFANY

Alex Morgan attended Diamond Bar High School, where she immediately attracted attention for her athletic abilities. For a time, Morgan and the South Korean singer Tiffany (originally Stephanie Young Hwang) attended the school together. Like Morgan, Tiffany was born in 1989 and brought up in Diamond Bar; however, the aspiring musician left Diamond Bar and moved to South Korea. There, her career took off with the girl group Girls' Generation and also as a solo artist.

Dev

MEANWHILE, IN SAN FRANCISCO . . .

Morgan was born close to Los Angeles on the same day that Devin Star Tailes was born in the city of Tracy, west of San Francisco. Now known by the stage name Dev, Tailes became a rapper and musician. In 2010, one of her songs was sampled by the band Far East Movement for the song "Like a G6." Following its success, she released her own single, "Bass Down Low," and her debut album, *The Night the Sun Came Up*. Before Tailes entered the limelight, during her high school years she was a promising swimmer.

Despite a left knee injury, Alex Morgan of the Portland Thorns enters the game against Western New York Flash during the second period of the 2013 National Women's Soccer League Championship at Sahlen's Stadium in Rochester, New York.

Mighty Mouse

14

THE TOMBOY

Alexandra ("Alex") Patricia Morgan was brought up in a loving family in Diamond Bar. The youngest of three daughters, she is very close to her older sisters, Jeni and Jeri. She had numerous friends, and many of them were really into sports. The Morgan family is well off and Alex always invited friends over to play in the pool, play video games, or take part in various ball games or other sports. She describes Diamond Bar as the "perfect place" in which to grow up.

In a YouTube video made by U.S. Soccer titled *Alex Morgan: Daughter of Diamond Bar*, Morgan says of herself: "I was the biggest tomboy. Everyone knows I'm competitive—I loved to beat all the boys. This was a time when you were still kind of even with the boys, they still hadn't surpassed you in athletic ability, so I was loving it—beating all the boys with sprinting, with soccer . . . anything."

Morgan's explosive pace was evident from an early age. For a time she was called "Mighty Mouse" because she ran so fast. She and her friends played basketball, tetherball, kickball, and other sports. Morgan smilingly maintains she was the "Tetherball Queen" of Maple Hill Elementary School. But soon soccer took over. Morgan's parents were her first coaches.

Screenshots of young Alex Morgan from U.S. Soccer's YouTube video about the player and her upbringing in Diamond Bar.

IN THE BEGINNING

The origins of soccer can be traced to nineteenth-century England. Various sports similar to soccer had long been played in England, but finally they were united under the aegis of the British Football Association. From England the sport spread across the world. The United States embraced soccer at the end of the century.

It so happened that a few years earlier, a closely related sport inspired by British rugby had taken root in the United States. This sport quickly became very popular in the United States and took on the name "football." When the so-called "association football" later traveled across the Atlantic it was dubbed "soccer." The name was simply extracted from the word *association*.

Soon after men began playing soccer in Europe, women also took the field. Soccer was widely played, and following the First World War (1914–18), women's soccer became so popular in Britain that tens of thousands of people flocked to observe the games. As a result, the men took action and attempted to stop the progress of women's soccer: women were forbidden to play on

SOME OF THE BIGGEST STARS OF WOMEN'S SOCCER OUTSIDE THE UNITED STATES IN RECENT DECADES

SUN WEN
China
Born 1973
With the Chinese national team
1990–2006
Games: 152
Goals: 106

BIRGIT PRINZ
Germany
Born 1977
With the German national team
1994–2011
Games: 214
Goals: 128

MARTA
Brazil
Born 1986
With the Brazilian national team
since 2002
Games: 73*
Goals: 82*

* As of October 2014.

traditional soccer fields. The same rule was instituted elsewhere. Women's soccer was systematically repressed and it was routinely claimed that soccer was "inappropriate" for women. The development of women's soccer therefore came to a halt for decades but finally began again in the latter part of the twentieth century. The popularity of the sport steadily increased around the world.

In the United States, women's soccer received a huge boost when Title IX, part of the Federal Education Amendments of 1972, was passed. It stipulated that schools were required to equally fund athletic programs for both genders. Even though attempts to found a women's professional league had gotten off to a rocky start, soccer flourished in schools, colleges, and universities. A national team was established and played its first game in 1985. A daring fighting spirit characterized the U.S. team from the very beginning, and it quickly entered the list of the world's greatest teams.

A women's game in Britain in 1914—no lack of spectators.

FIRST WORLD CUP GOLD

The first Women's World Cup was held in China in 1991. The U.S. team won all its games—most of them confidently—including a complete lashing of the German team in a 5–2 victory in the semifinal.

JULIE FOUDY
Born 1971 in San Diego, CA
With the national team 1987–2004
Games: 271
Goals: 45

JOY FAWCETT
Born 1968 in Inglewood, CA
With the national team 1987–2004
Games: 239
Goals: 27

1991 Women's World Cup Final
*November 30, 1991
Tianhe Stadium, Guanghou, China
Attendance: 65,000*

USA VS. NORWAY

2–1

GOALS

USA: Akers 20', 78'   Norway: Medalen 29'

USA's Lineup
Harvey (goalkeeper)
Biefeld – Werden – Hamilton
Hamm – Higgins – Foudy – Lilly
Heinrichs – Akers – Jennings

Coach: Anson Dorrance

Midfielder Joy Fawcett and defender Julie Foudy formed the defensive backbone of the strong U.S. team during the 1990s.

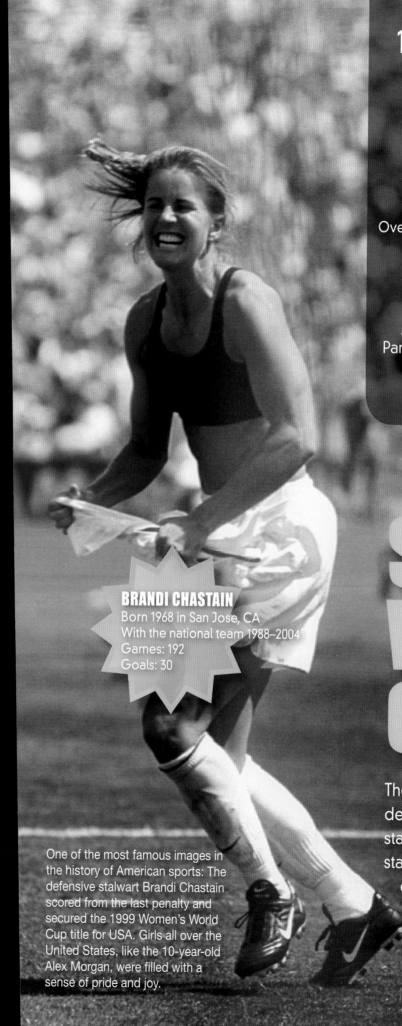

1999 Women's World Cup Final
July 10, 1999
Rose Bowl, Pasadena, CA
Attendance: 90,185

USA VS. CHINA
0–0 (5–4*)

*After extra time and penalties.
Overbeck, Fawcett, Lilly, Hamm, and Chastain scored.
Scurry saved one Chinese penalty.

USA's Lineup
Scurry (goalkeeper)
Overbeck – Chastain – Fawcett – Sobrero
Akers (Whalen 91') – Hamm – Lilly – Foudy
Parlow (MacMillan 57') – Milbrett (Venturini 115')

Coach: Tony DiCiccio

BRANDI CHASTAIN
Born 1968 in San Jose, CA
With the national team 1988–2004
Games: 192
Goals: 30

One of the most famous images in the history of American sports: The defensive stalwart Brandi Chastain scored from the last penalty and secured the 1999 Women's World Cup title for USA. Girls all over the United States, like the 10-year-old Alex Morgan, were filled with a sense of pride and joy.

SECOND WORLD CUP GOLD

The 1996 U.S. Olympic champions easily defeated their opponents during the group stage of the World Cup. During the knockout stage, the U.S. team managed to defeat extremely tough opposition (Germany and Brazil) and reached the final against China. The difficult game was not decided until the very last kick.

THE ROLE MODELS

The United States boasts a number of skillful players in women's soccer. These four dangerous forwards all inspired the young Alex Morgan.

MICHELLE AKERS

Born 1966 in Santa Clara, CA
Member of national team 1985–2000
Games: 153
Goals: 105

Akers

Michelle Akers grew up in Seattle. Tall and athletic, she was an aggressive forward who later changed her position to midfield. She was the top scorer in the first Women's World Cup in 1991, with a total of 10 goals in six games. Akers scored both goals for the U.S. team in the final, securing a 2–1 victory over Norway. She was also a gold medalist at the 1996 Olympics in Atlanta.

Akers contributed significantly to the 1999 World Cup winning team and was included in the tournament's All-Star Team.

In 1999, she was voted FIFA Player of the Century, together with China's Sun Wen.

KRISTINE LILLY

Born 1971 in New York, NY
Member of national team 1987–2010
Games: 352
Goals: 130

In a remarkable career, Kristine Lilly won two World Cup gold medals and two Olympic gold medals. Lilly is one of only four players—and the sole woman—who have played in five World Cup tournaments. She was an ever-present attacking midfielder on the U.S. team for more than 20 years, and she holds the record for most international appearances: 352.

Lilly

MIA HAMM

Born 1972 in Selma, AL
Member of national team 1987–2004
Games: 275
Goals: 158

Mia Hamm was introduced to soccer in Italy, where her father was stationed for a time with the U.S. Air Force. Hamm began playing for the U.S. national team at 15, still the youngest athlete ever to play for it. An extremely prolific goalscorer, Hamm was a member of the victorious U.S. teams at both the 1991 and 1999 World Cups, and was also on the World Cup All-Star team in 1999. Moreover, Hamm became an Olympic gold medalist in 1996 and 2004.

Hamm garnered numerous awards throughout her career and was chosen as the FIFA Female Player of the Year in 2001 and 2002, the first two years that the award was given. In 2004, Hamm and Michelle Akers were the only women on FIFA's list of the 125 greatest soccer players in history, assembled by the soccer legend Pelé.

TIFFENY MILBRETT

Born 1972 in Portland, OR
Member of national team 1991–2006
Games: 204
Goals: 100

Tiffeny Milbrett was a powerful forward. She won gold medals with the U.S. team at the 1996 Atlanta Olympics and the 1999 World Cup, where she was the leading U.S. goalscorer.

Milbrett

Hamm

CAREER

Alex Morgan attended the University of California, Berkeley, from 2007 to 2010. Despite the demands of playing soccer for the California Golden Bears, she graduated a semester early with a degree in political economy. Morgan was the top goalscorer during the time she played with the team and accumulated numerous awards.

Since leaving the Golden Bears, Morgan has played with teams across the United States. Everywhere Morgan goes she racks up goals with her speed, agility, and energy. In spring 2013, she joined a new team, the Portland Thorns, which participated in the newly founded National Women's Soccer League. Fans of women's soccer in the United States hope that the NWSL will finally establish an enduring league that will facilitate the growth of the game in their country. And Alex Morgan will do her utmost to make that happen! Morgan scored important goals for her team during the first season, and in the final of the championship game she assisted Christine Sinclair's winning goal during stoppage time.

Despite Morgan's ambition while playing with individual teams, it quickly became clear that her success would be no less with the national team.

Alex's teams

Team	City	Season
West Coast FC	Los Angeles	2008–09
California Storm	Sacramento	2010
Pali Blues	Los Angeles	2010
Western New York Flash	Buffalo	2011
Seattle Sounders Women	Seattle	2012
Portland Thorns	Portland	2013–

Morgan attends the debut of designer jewelry company lia sophia's Boudika Red Carpet Collection during New York Fashion Week in September 2011.

BABY HORSE

Alex Morgan was on the team that competed in the U-20 Women's World Cup in Chile in November and December 2008. Morgan scored the first goal of the U.S. team's first victory in the tournament, a 3–0 defeat over France. She scored a total of four goals and showed great skill, along with another newcomer, Sydney Leroux. Fittingly, Morgan and Leroux each scored a goal in the final, which the U.S. team won against North Korea 2–1.

Morgan played in her first game with a senior national team on March 31, 2010, when she entered as a substitute in a match against Mexico that took place in Salt Lake City, Utah. She scored her first goal on October 6, 2010, in a friendly game against China in Chester, Pennsylvania. The goal equalized the game, which ended in a 1–1 draw.

Six weeks later, on November 20, 2010, Morgan scored an extremely important goal. The U.S. team experienced unexpected difficulties in securing its position at the 2011 World Cup and was forced to undergo a double-round playoff with Italy. In the tense first match in Padua, Italy, the teams seemed destined for a 0–0 draw when Morgan entered the field in the 86th minute. Four minutes into stoppage time she managed to break the deadlock with a well-taken goal. She even managed to score with her right foot this time! The goal moved the U.S. team closer to qualifying for a place in the 2011 World Cup, and after they secured it in the second playoff round, Morgan of course accompanied the team to the tournament in Germany.

It was now clear that a future star was born. Morgan immediately became popular and respected, by both her fans and her teammates. She was often referred to as "Baby Horse" for her pace, energy, and competitiveness. The nickname, though, is rarely used now.

FABULOUS GOAL!

Morgan's goal in the final of the U-20 World Cup on December 7, 2008, against North Korea was fabulous and soared across the world on the wings of the Internet. The goal was named the best goal of the tournament, and FIFA later chose it as the second-best goal of the year, regardless of player age or gender. The goal demonstrated the diversity of Morgan's strength. She received the ball close to midfield far out on the right wing, shook off two defenders, and went alone up against two others before she blasted a beautiful left-foot shot from outside the penalty area past the defenseless North Korean goalkeeper.

Conditions were not optimal when Alex Morgan played her first match with the U.S. national team, but she did not waver. Morgan is known for never giving up.

Alex Morgan retweeted

Portland Thorns FC @ThornsFC · Sep 12
Rio Tinto Stadium. Mexico. A fun reflection by @AlexMorgan13 on her first #USWNT cap. ow.ly/Brhwv #BAONPDX

Keelin Winter celebrates with Alex Morgan after her decisive goal against North Korea. Nikki Marshall runs toward them, but North Korean defender Kim Chun Hui is devastated.

WORLD CUP 2011

Date	Opponent	Results			U.S. Goalscorers
June 28	North Korea	2–0		W	Cheney, Buehler
July 2	Colombia	3–0		W	O'Reilly, Rapinoe, Lloyd
July 6	Sweden	1–2		L	Wambach
July 10	Brazil	2–2*	5–3*	W	Brazil own goal, Wambach
July 13	France	3–1		W	Cheney, Wambach, Morgan
July 17	Japan	2–2**	1–3**	L	Morgan, Wambach

* After extra time and penalties. Boxx, Lloyd, Wambach, Rapinoe, and Krieger all scored for the USA.
** After extra times and penalties. Boxx, Lloyd, and Heath missed for the USA; only Wambach scored.

FIRST TASTE OF GLORY

Alex Morgan was the youngest member of the powerful U.S. team that took part in the 2011 Women's World Cup in Germany. (She turned 22 during the tournament.) It was therefore natural that she would begin on the bench. Morgan entered as a substitute in the first match of the group stage and again in the third when the United States unexpectedly lost to the tougher Swedish team. Coincidentally, Sweden is the home country of U.S. coach Pia Sundhage.

Morgan also played in a greatly competitive match against Brazil in the quarterfinals. Following a heavy battle, the U.S. team came out victorious even though the team was short by one player. USA then got into a tight spot during its semifinal game against France but later managed to turn its luck around. Morgan's skill and fighting spirit played a major role when she scored her first World Cup goal in the 82nd minute. It was a classic Alex Morgan goal: she received a pass through the defense, gained control of the ball, and fired an incisive shot over the French goalkeeper. In this way, Alex Morgan helped secure the U.S. team's place in the World Cup final.

Alex Morgan celebrates scoring the U.S. team's first goal during the Women's World Cup final match against Japan.

Alex Morgan certainly made her mark in the 2011 Women's World Cup final against Japan. The Japanese team won a startling victory over Germany in the quarterfinals and then over Sweden in the semifinals. The U.S. team was favored and had the upper hand in the first half, but did not manage to score a goal. There was one thing missing: Alex Morgan.

When Morgan entered in the second half, she immediately aroused an increased offensive thrust and fighting spirit in the team. In the 69th minute, Morgan received a brilliant long pass from Megan Rapinoe, controlled the ball extremely well, and blasted an unstoppable shot with her famed left foot into the Japanese net. The U. S. women's team seemed to be on the road toward a third World Cup gold.

Japan, however, equalized after an unusual mistake by the U.S. defense, and the game went into extra time. Again, Morgan did her utmost for the cause. She made a great pass to Abby Wambach, who delivered the ball into the goal. But with only three minutes left, Japan once again equalized. The game was finally decided by penalties and the U.S. team lost.

The defeat was a great disappointment for the ambitious U.S. team, but for Morgan it was still a rewarding experience. And another chance would arrive four years later!

THE FIRST

Alex Morgan (center) looks dejected after the Women's World Cup final match between Japan and USA at the FIFA World Cup Stadium on July 17, 2011, in Frankfurt am Main, Germany.

FINAL

HOW TALL IS SHE?

HEIGHT UNDER THE BAR: 8 FEET

CRISTIANO RONALDO
6' 1"

MIA HAMM
5' 5"

MARTA
5' 3"

Height isn't everything in soccer. In fact, it matters less than in most other sports. Still, it is interesting to see how Alex Morgan compares to some of the other legends of women's soccer—and a few men!

LIONEL
MESSI
5' 7"

ALEX
MORGAN
5' 7"

HOPE SOLO
5' 9"

ABBY WAMBACH
Born 1980 in Rochester, NY
Member of national team since 2001
Games (as of November 2014): 228
Goals: 177

Abby Wambach (right) was named the 2012 FIFA Women's World
Player of the Year. Brazil's Marta (left) and Alex Morgan (center) were
ranked second and third, respectively.

ABBY AND ALEX

Abby Wambach is an extremely strong and competitive goalscorer. Wambach has already won two Olympic gold medals and is looking to add the World Cup medal to her impressive collection of awards. On June 21, 2013, she broke Mia Hamm's long-standing record as the top goalscorer of the U.S. team when she scored against South Korea in a friendly scrimmage. Since then, Wambach has considerably expanded her tally of goals. She scored five goals at the 2012 Olympics and was voted the 2012 FIFA World Player of the Year, the first U.S. player since Mia Hamm a decade earlier. In third place came her new striking partner, Alex Morgan.

Abby will carry the torch for the U.S. team for many years to come. One can assume that the duo will continue to rack up goals.

Alex Morgan and Abby Wambach are an unstoppable pair on the front lines of the U.S. team. Morgan has assisted 16 of Wambach's goals!

ALEX MORGAN AT THE WHITE HOUSE

Alex Morgan visited the White House in October 2011 as part of First Lady Michelle Obama's Let's Move! initiative. Assisted by members of the United States Women's National Team, Mrs. Obama hosted a soccer clinic held on the South Lawn of the White House. Let's Move! was started by Mrs. Obama as a way to promote healthier lifestyles in children across the country.

Representatives of the USWNT with First Lady Michelle Obama. Left to right: General Manager Cheryl Bailey (now executive director of the National Women's Soccer League), Becky Sauerbrunn, Rachel Buehler, Nicole Barnhart, Michelle Obama, Alex Morgan, Lori Lindsey, and Kelley O'Hara.

EN ROUTE TO THE OLYMPICS

As the U.S. team prepared for the 2012 London Olympics, Alex became a regular starter on the front line, usually alongside veteran Abby Wambach.

Morgan was a prominent presence at the CONCACAF* qualifying tournament held in January in the Canadian city of Vancouver. Amy Rodriguez and Sydney Leroux reigned supreme in the first two games, in which the U.S. team faced relatively easy opposition. However, Morgan came to the fore as the opponents grew stronger. In the semifinals she scored the third goal in a 3–0 victory over Costa Rica. And in the final against the host country, she practically ran the show. Morgan scored two goals in a magnificent display of skill and set up an additional two for Wambach. The U.S. defense, meanwhile, managed to control Canada's outstanding striker Christine Sinclair. In fact, the U.S. team didn't concede a single goal during the entire tournament.

Canada's best player gracefully accepted the 4–0 defeat: "I think they showed tonight why they are the best team in the world."

There was no stopping the girl from Diamond Bar on the way to the Olympics. Morgan scored an incredible 17 goals in the first half of 2012.

And then the Games properly began.

* See glossary, page 60.

Alex Morgan (#13) celebrates with Megan Rapinoe after scoring against Canada during the first half of championship action in the 2012 CONCACAF Women's Olympic Qualifying Tournament. The contest was held at BC Place on January 29, 2012, in Vancouver, British Columbia, Canada.

CONCACAF 2012
Women's Olympic Qualifying Tournament

Date	Opponent	Results		U.S. Goalscorers
Jan. 20	Dominican Rep.	14–0	W	Wambach 2, Lloyd, Buehler, O'Reilly 3, Heath, A. Rodriguez 5, Cheney
Jan. 22	Guatemala	13–0	W	Wambach 2, Cheney, A. Rodriguez, Lloyd, Lindsey, Leroux 5, Rapinoe, Morgan
Jan. 24	Mexico	4–0	W	Lloyd 3, O'Reilly
Jan. 27	Costa Rica	3–0	W	Heath, Lloyd, Morgan

ALEX TO THE RESCUE!

The prospects were bleak 14 minutes into the first game of the Olympics' group stage. The score was 2–0 for France. But the U.S. women rallied together. Boosted by the skills of Alex Morgan, who scored two goals out of four, the U.S. team ultimately won 4–2. Alex was a constant threat with her speed and fighting spirit.

Next, the U.S. team confidently defeated Colombia 3–0, then overcame the spirited North Korean team in the final group game. Abby Wambach scored the game's only goal, with Morgan providing the assist.

In the quarterfinals, the U.S. team breezily defeated New Zealand 2–0. However, the semifinal match against continental rival Canada was destined for the history books. Canada's Christine Sinclair scored a hat trick that placed her team in the lead, but each time USA responded, and the game went into extra time. In the 122nd minute penalties loomed, but the resolute Morgan scored a winning goal with a strong header from a cross delivered by Heather O'Reilly.

Alex Morgan scored the winning goal in extra time during the 2012 Olympic semifinal match between Canada and USA on Day 10 of the Games at Old Trafford Stadium in Manchester, England.

London Olympics 2012

Date	Opponent	Results		U.S. Goalscorers
July 25	France	4–2	W	Wambach, Morgan 2, Lloyd
July 28	Colombia	3–0	W	Rapinoe, Wambach, Lloyd
July 31	North Korea	1–0	W	Wambach
Aug. 3	New Zealand	2–0	W	Wambach, Leroux
Aug. 6	Canada	4–3*	W	Rapinoe 2, Wambach, Morgan
Aug. 9	Japan	2–1	W	Lloyd 2

* After extra time.

THE GREATEST PRIZE

More than 80,000 people gathered at Wembley, Britain's national football (soccer) stadium, on August 9, 2012, to witness the battle between USA and Japan over the women's gold medal. Only eight minutes into the game, Alex Morgan tenaciously controlled the ball while pressed by the Japanese defense, then managed a brave cross that Carli Lloyd converted. Lloyd later added another goal and sealed the win, in spite of a late Japanese goal. And so the U.S. team won its third consecutive Olympic gold medal. Morgan deserved to be extremely proud, having contributed to the team's success throughout the Games.

Alex Morgan celebrates her Olympic gold medal after the U.S. team defeated Japan by a score of 2–1 to win the final match at Wembley Stadium on August 9, 2012, in London, England.

teresa yeager

What is your biggest achievement?

Alex Morgan

Receiving my Olympic Gold Medal. I am forever an Olympic Gold Medalist.

46   17

FAVORITES

Alex replies to her fans' questions on the Web. A sample of her lively answers reveal her interests and personality—at once boisterous and thoughtful.

Franklin Mendez

If you can meet any famous person in the world, who would it be and why?

Alex Morgan

Muhammad Ali in his prime, to learn how he became such a competitor, what his thoughts were.

♥ 65   ➦ 19

May 25, 1965: World heavyweight champion Muhammad Ali knocks out Sonny Liston in the first round of Ali's return title fight.

Sandra Martinez

What is your favorite movie?

Alex Morgan

The Bind Side and Catch Me If You Can.

♥ 56   ➦ 16

42

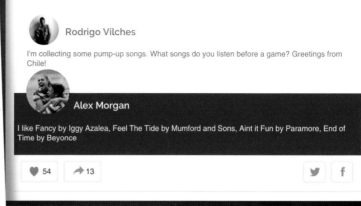

Rodrigo Vilches

I'm collecting some pump-up songs. What songs do you listen before a game? Greetings from Chile!

Alex Morgan

I like Fancy by Iggy Azalea, Feel The Tide by Mumford and Sons, Aint it Fun by Paramore, End of Time by Beyonce

♥ 54   ➤ 13   🐦 f

Joel Werner

What is your favorite place to travel around the world ?

Alex Morgan

Anywhere with clear blue water.

♥ 42   ➤ 8

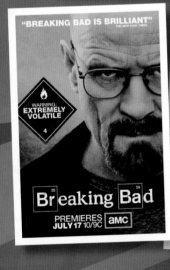

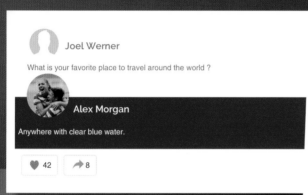

Kaka#22

What is your favorite TV series?

Alex Morgan

Too hard to pick 1! Breaking Bad (just finished it!), Modern Family, American Ninja Warrior.

♥ 33   ➤ 45   🐦 f

Alex Morgan @alexmorgan13 · Aug 8

They gave me number 13 for my breakfast order and the total was $13. I think it's time to play the lottery! #itsagoodmorning

↩   ⇄ 498   ★ 3.4K   ···

MORE FAVORITES

Kendall

If you could be any animal you want, what animal would you choose and why?

Alex Morgan

Snow Leopard or a Cheetah

♥ 23   ➤ 3

isabel

Favorite singer?

Alex Morgan

Tie between Ellie Goulding and Ben Howard.

♥ 66   ➤ 10   🐦   f

Nick Caesar

If you weren't a soccer player what profession would you choose?

Alex Morgan

I've had a dream of becoming a professional soccer player since I was 7 years old. If not for soccer, I'd probably be involved with animals in some way. We are their voice, and it's something that I deeply care about.

♥ 99   ➤ 19   🐦   f

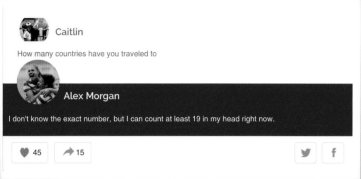

Caitlin

How many countries have you traveled to

Alex Morgan

I don't know the exact number, but I can count at least 19 in my head right now.

♥ 45   → 15   𝕏   f

Alex Morgan looks on during the U.S. team's first round match against North Korea in the London 2012 Olympic Games.

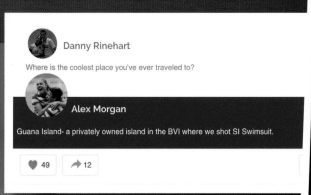

Danny Rinehart

Where is the coolest place you've ever traveled to?

Alex Morgan

Guana Island- a privately owned island in the BVI where we shot SI Swimsuit.

♥ 49   → 12

View at nightfall from Camanoe Island over Guana Island and Tortola, all part of the British Virgin Islands in the Caribbean.

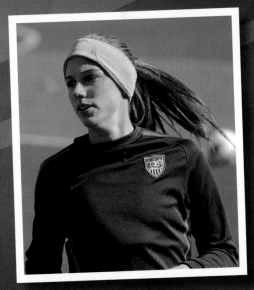

Alex Morgan @alexmorgan13 · Aug 25

I've lived in so many cities I think I can officially add professional packer to my résumé.

↩   ⟲ 199   ★ 1.6K   •••

Alex Morgan playing for the United States Women's National Team in Frisco, Texas, in February 2012.

THE WRITER

Alex Morgan has many talents. She graduated from the University of California, Berkeley, with a degree in political economy, and in 2012 she signed a book contract with Simon & Schuster, one of America's most significant publishing companies. Morgan has written a series of middle-grade novels that revolve around four friends who play soccer and who deal with everyday events that kids experience. The series is titled "The Kicks," and the first book, *Saving the Team*, was published in March 2014. The novel debuted at number seven on the *New York Times* Best Seller list for Children's Middle Grade. *Sabotage Season* followed in June of the same year, and the third book, *Win or Lose,* hit the shelves in August.

The books have been well received and are thought to exhibit, along with an entertaining story, how a positive attitude, optimism, and self-confidence reward everyone with success.

SYNOPSIS OF *SAVING THE TEAM*

Twelve-year-old Devin loves to play soccer. If she hadn't just left Connecticut to move across the country, she would have been named seventh-grade captain on her school soccer team.

But now that Devin is starting seventh grade in Kentville, California, all bets are off. After all, some of the best players on the U.S. National Team come from California. She's sure to have stiff competition. Or so she thinks.

When Devin shows up for tryouts, she discovers that the Kentville Kangaroos—otherwise known as the Kicks—are an absolute mess. Their coach couldn't care less whether the girls win or lose. And Devin is easily one of the most talented players.

The good news is, Devin quickly makes friends with funny, outgoing Jessi; shy but sweet Zoe; and klutzy Emma. Can Devin and her newfound friends pull together and save the team from itself?

Alex Morgan promotes her new book, *The Kicks: Saving the Team,* at Bookends Bookstore on May 7, 2013, in Ridgewood, New Jersey.

THE MODEL

Alex Morgan arrives at the Los Angeles premiere of *The Twilight Saga: Breaking Dawn — Part 2* at Nokia Theatre L.A. Live on November 12, 2012, in Los Angeles, California.

Morgan attends "D.J. Night with Freida Pinto" in support of Girl Rising, a campaign to promote the education of girls worldwide. The event, hosted by *Vanity Fair* and L'Oréal Paris, took place at Teddy's at the Hollywood Roosevelt Hotel on February 19, 2013, in Los Angeles, California.

Morgan walks the runway to songs from UbiSoft's *Just Dance 4* at the Tumbler and Tipsy by Michael Kuluva fashion show, held at STYLE360 in the Metropolitan Pavilion on September 11, 2012, in New York City.

These photos represent a few of Morgan's ads for Nike. She has also signed endorsement deals with Panasonic, the Coca-Cola Company, Bank of America, and other companies.

ALEX MORGAN AND THE ADS

A popular soccer star like Alex Morgan is, of course, sought-after by advertisers.

CARLI LLOYD

Lloyd is among the older players on the U.S. team but she is a true role model with her spirit and technical skill. Although Lloyd is a midfielder, she scores many goals and has lived a true dream by landing the decisive goals in two Olympics finals in a row: first, in 2008 (1–0 in overtime against Brazil) and then two goals against Japan in 2012.

Carli Lloyd (front) and Alex Morgan celebrate Lloyd's second goal against Japan in the final game of the 2012 Olympics in London.

CARLI LLOYD
Born 1982 in New Jersey

SYDNEY LEROUX

Although Abby Wambach (see page 32) is still at the top of her game, other fantastic forwards have entered the world stage who will lead the goal-scoring march of the U.S. team in the coming years. At the forefront is Sydney Leroux—agile, highly spirited, and an eager goalscorer. Leroux was born in Canada but she has an American father. Leroux and Morgan first crossed paths when they participated together in the 2008 U–20 Women's World Cup in Chile, where Leroux showcased her tremendous skill by winning both the Golden Shoe and the Golden Ball.

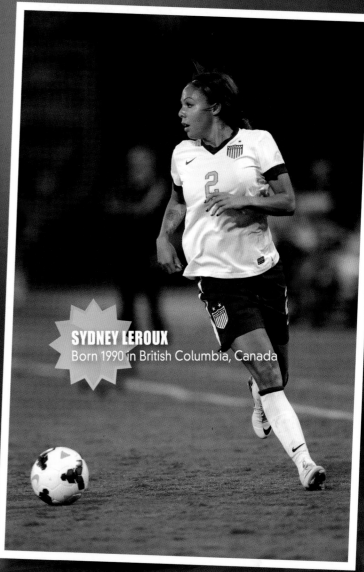

SYDNEY LEROUX
Born 1990 in British Columbia, Canada

AMY RODRIGUEZ
Born 1987 in California

CHRISTEN PRESS
Born 1988 in California

OTHER FORWARDS

Amy Rodriguez is a powerful and speedy player who can assume most roles of the forward and always delivers. Fellow Californian Christen Press is a more recent addition to the U.S. team but is already racking up goals.

ALEX & COMPANY

HOPE SOLO

Wherever the headstrong goalkeeper Hope Solo goes, controversy follows. However, one thing is indisputable: her goalkeeping ability. Solo's unwavering fighting spirit and professionalism make her the most successful goalkeeper of the U.S. team. In the fall of 2014, Solo set a new U.S. record for shutouts (not conceding a goal).

HOPE SOLO
Born 1981 in Washington

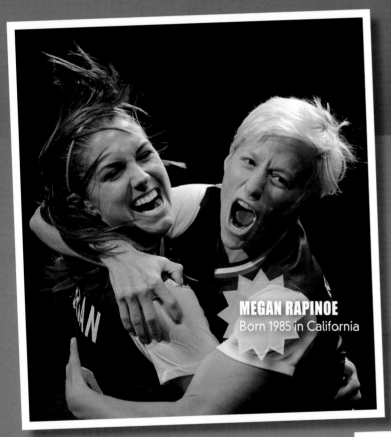

MEGAN RAPINOE
Born 1985 in California

MEGAN RAPINOE

Megan Rapinoe is a dynamic and offensive midfielder who made a vast contribution to the outstanding performance of the U.S. team in the 2012 Olympics. Rapinoe always plays with great passion and energy.

OTHER MIDFIELDERS

HEATHER O'REILLY
Born 1985 in New Jersey

TOBIN HEATH
Born 1988 in New Jersey

LAUREN HOLIDAY
Born 1987 in Indiana

SHANNON BOXX
Born 1977 in California

THE CAPTAIN

An important factor in the performance of the U.S. team has been its rigorously organized and resilient defense. Captain of the team since 2008, Christie Rampone has led the field for the most part. She was a member of the victorious 1999 World Cup team and she would surely love to end her illustrious career by securing another World Cup victory in 2015. Rampone will celebrate her 40th birthday during the tournament.

CHRISTIE RAMPONE
Born 1975 in Florida

PARTNERS IN DEFENSE

BECKY SAUERBRUNN
Born 1985 in Missouri

ALI KRIEGER
Born 1984 in Virginia

MEGHAN KLINGENBERG
Born 1988 in Pennsylvania

KELLEY O'HARA
Born 1988 in Georgia

RACHEL VAN HOLLEBEKE (NÉE BUEHLER)
Born 1985 in California

THE FIANCÉ

On December 9, 2013, Morgan announced to her fans on Twitter that she was officially engaged to Servando Carrasco. He is, perhaps unsurprisingly, also a soccer player. Carrasco plays mainly as a defensive midfielder.

Carrasco was born on August 13, 1988. He is thus one year older than Alex. Although he was born in San Diego, California, Carrasco lived with his parents and older sister in Tijuana, Mexico, until he was seven years old. At that time, the family moved permanently to San Diego. In 2007, Carrasco accepted a scholarship to the University of California, Berkeley, and played for the California Golden Bears for the next three years. While playing for the team he met Morgan, who was also playing for the Golden Bears.

The Seattle Sounders signed Carrasco in 2011; he played with the team for two years. Morgan played for the Seattle Sounders Women for a short spell in 2012. In 2013 Carrasco joined the Houston Dynamo. Despite playing for different teams in different cities, Carrasco and Morgan still try to meet at every opportunity in order to nurture their relationship.

servando + alex

Alex Morgan ✔
@alexmorgan13　🐦 **Follow**

Couldn't be happier. #lifeisgood

12:00 AM - 10 Dec 2013

6,840 RETWEETS **17,015** FAVORITES

THE FUTURE

Alex Morgan signs autographs for fans after the U.S. team's international friendly match against Australia at The Home Depot Center on September 16, 2012, in Carson, California. USA defeated Australia 2–1.

AND THE FANS

If Alex Morgan can avoid serious injuries, chances are good that she will become one of the leading soccer players of the next decade. Morgan already numbers among the world's greatest, as her popularity clearly shows. She is a role model to numerous young soccer players around the globe— not only girls but boys, too.

Glossary

FIFA: The International Football Federation (Fédération Internationale de Football Association), the governing body of soccer (football), beach soccer, and futsal (indoor soccer) throughout the world. FIFA organizes the main international competitions, including the World Cup, for both women and men. As of 2014, 209 countries were full members of FIFA, through one of the six continental federations: AFC (Asia), CAF (Africa), COMNEBOL (South America), OFC (Oceania), UEFA (Europe), and CONCACAF.

CONCACAF: The Confederation of North, Central American, and Caribbean Association Football (soccer). The North and Central American members (3 and 7, respectively) are all full-fledged members of FIFA, but the Caribbean Zone comprises 25 FIFA members and 6 territories outside FIFA.

World Cup: The world championship competition of soccer, held every four years. The men's World Cup was held for the first time in 1930, won by Uruguay. As of 2014 Brazil has won the World Cup five times, Germany and Italy four times each, Uruguay and Argentina twice each, and England, France, and Spain once. The women's edition was first held in 1991 and won by the USA. As of 2014, the U.S. team has won the Women's World Cup twice, as has Germany. Norway and Japan have each won once.

Striker: A forward player positioned closest to the opposing goal who has the primary role of receiving the ball from teammates and delivering it to the goal, or assisting teammates in doing just that. Alex Morgan usually assists almost as many goals as she scores herself!

Winger: A player who keeps to the margins of the field, receives the ball from midfielders or defenders, and sends it forward to where the strikers await.

Offensive midfielder: A player positioned behind the team's forwards who seeks to take the ball through the opposing defense, where she either passes to the strikers or attempts a goal herself. This position is sometimes called "number ten" in reference to the Brazilian genius Pelé, who more or less created the position and wore shirt number 10.

Defensive midfielder: Usually plays in front of her team's defense. This player's central role is to break the offense of the opposing team and deliver the ball to the forwards of her own team. The contribution of defensive midfielders is not always obvious, but they nevertheless play an important part in the game.

Central midfielder: The role of the central midfielder is divided between offense and defense, but mainly she seeks to secure the center of the field for her team. Box-to-box midfielders are versatile players who possess such strength and oversight that they constantly spring between the penalty areas.

Fullbacks (either leftbacks or rightbacks): Players who defend the sides of the field, near their own goal, but who also dash up the field and overlap with wingers in order to lob the ball into the opponent's goal. Fullbacks are sometimes titled wingbacks, if they are expected to play a bigger role in the offense.

Centerbacks: These players are the primary defenders of their teams, and are two or three in number depending on formation. The purpose of the centerback is first and foremost to prevent the opponents from scoring, and then to send the ball toward the center.

Sweeper: The original purpose of the sweeper was to stay behind her defending teammates and "sweep up" the ball if they happened to lose it, but also to take the ball forward. The position of the sweeper has now been replaced by defensive midfielders.

Goalkeeper: Prevents the opponent's goals and is the only player who is allowed to use her hands!

CHOOSE THE TEAM

Coach:

_____

Who do you want playing with Alex Morgan? Choose a team for her. Don't forget the coach! You can choose any player you want, female or male, past or present. You can even choose yourself or your friends!

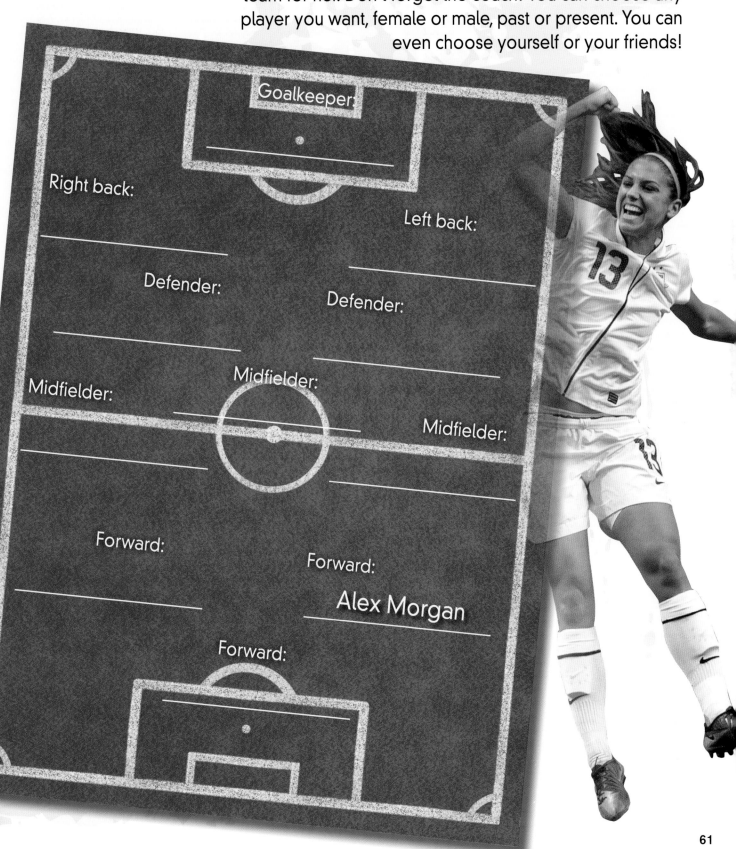

Goalkeeper:
_____

Right back:
_____

Left back:
_____

Defender:
_____

Defender:
_____

Midfielder:
_____

Midfielder:
_____

Midfielder:
_____

Forward:
_____

Forward:
Alex Morgan

Forward:
_____

YOU SCORE A BRILLIANT GOAL WHEN FINALLY PLAYING FOR THE U-20 TEAM. YOU ARE MOBBED BY JOURNALISTS AND MUST WAIT ONE ROUND.

10

YOU TAKE PART IN THE WORLD CUP BUT THE U.S. TEAM FAILS TO WIN GOLD. GO BACK 3 PLACES.

YOU ARE DROPPED TO THE BENCH IN THE RUN-UP TO THE OLYMPICS. WARM THE BENCH FOR 1 ROUND.

8

YOU ARE CALLED TO THE U.S. U-20 WOMEN'S NATIONAL TEAM, BUT INJURY PREVENTS YOU FROM TAKING PART. GO BACK 2 PLACES.

Help Alex Win!

YOU SCORE YOUR FIRST GOAL FOR THE GOLDEN BEARS. GO FORWARD 4 PLACES.

13

YOU ATTEND UC BERKELEY BUT GET LOST IN THE CORRIDORS. WAIT ONE ROUND WHILE YOU FIND YOUR WAY.

5

YOU SCORE TWO GOALS AND PROVIDE TWO ASSISTS IN A CONCACAF FINAL. STRIDE FORWARD 3 PLACES.

YOU GRADUATE FROM DIAMOND BAR HIGH SCHOOL AS THE SCHOOL'S BEST SOCCER PLAYER. ROLL AGAIN.

YOU SCORE A HAT TRICK AND MIA HAMM PHONES TO CONGRATULATE YOU. ROLL AGAIN.

2

KICK OFF

THE ALEX MORGAN BOARD GAME!